SCARY STATES (OF MIND)

HORROR IN NORTH CAROLINA

by Simon Rose

Consultant: Debbie Felton
Professor of Classics
University of Massachusetts
Amherst, Massachusetts

BEARPORT PUBLISHING

New York, New York

Credits

Cover, © Bobkeenan Photography/Shutterstock, © Clever Captures's/Shutterstock, and © warnsweet's/Shutterstock; TOC, © samray/Shutterstock; 4–5, © Halfpoint/Shutterstock, © samray/Shutterstock, and © Kanoksak Dounglaor/Shutterstock; 7T, © Lario Tus/Shutterstock; 7B, © Strange Carolinas; 8, © Francisco Caravana/Shutterstock and © Lario Tus/Shutterstock; 9, © Chris Hocker/Strange Carolinas.com; 10–11, © Ken Schulze/Shutterstock; 11T, © Bridgeman Images; 11B, © Jill Lang/Shutterstock; 12, © Lee Snider Photo Images/Shutterstock; 13, © joel zatz/Alamy; 14, © faestock/Shutterstock; 15, © Ken Howard/Alamy; 17, © Smolina Marianna/Shutterstock and © faestock/Shutterstock; 19, © THEPALMER/iStock and © Neosiam992465/Shutterstock; 20, © Ollyy/Shutterstock; 20–21, © Frentusha/iStock; 23, © Clever Captures/Shutterstock; 24, © reptiles4all/Shutterstock.

Publisher: Kenn Goin
Senior Editor: Joyce Tavolacci
Creative Director: Spencer Brinker
Photo Researcher: Thomas Persano
Cover: Kim Jones

Library of Congress Cataloging-in-Publication Data in process at time of publication (2020)
Library of Congress Control Number: 2019007177
ISBN-13: 978-1-64280-519-2 (library binding)

For more information, write to Bearport Publishing Company, Inc., 45 West 21st Street, Suite 3B, New York, New York 10010. Printed in the United States of America.

10 9 8 7 6 5 4 3 2 1

CONTENTS

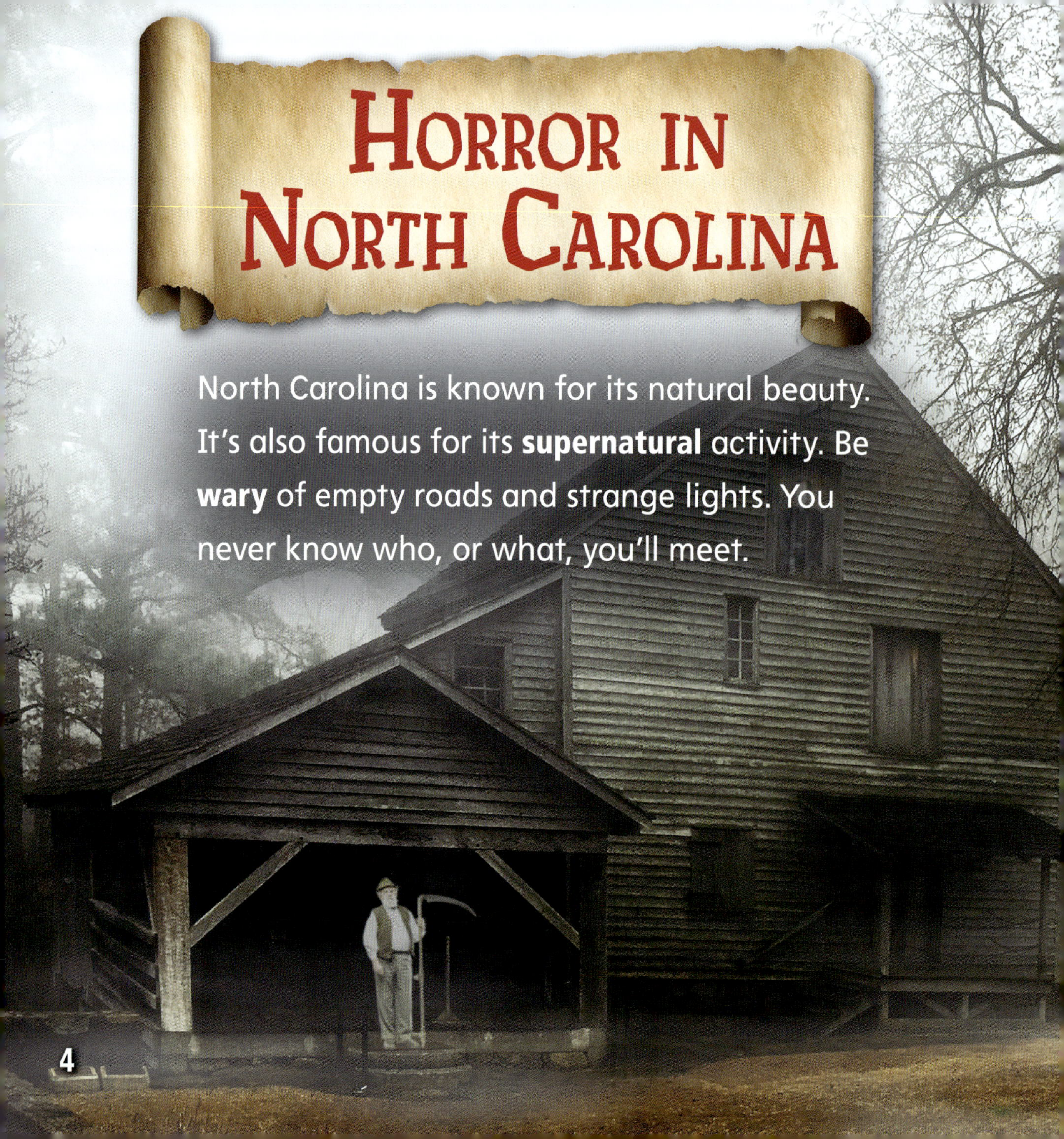

Horror in North Carolina

North Carolina is known for its natural beauty. It's also famous for its **supernatural** activity. Be **wary** of empty roads and strange lights. You never know who, or what, you'll meet.

Get ready to read four scary stories about North Carolina. Turn the page . . . if you dare.

The Woman in White

Lydia's Bridge, Greensboro

On rainy nights near a bridge in Greensboro, drivers sometimes see a young woman in a white dress. Many drivers offer the woman a ride. She gets in the back seat. When the drivers pull up to her house, the woman has **vanished** from the car!

The bridge in Greensboro is called Lydia's Bridge.

One shocked driver got out of his car and knocked on the door of the house. An old woman answered. The driver told her what had happened. The woman said she had heard this story before. She showed the man a photograph of her daughter, Lydia.

The man almost **fainted.** It was the same woman who had gotten into his car!

The driver learned that Lydia had died in a car accident by the bridge in 1923. After all these years, is she still trying to get home?

A Headless Pirate

Teach's Hole, Ocracoke Island

Teach's Hole is a small waterway near Ocracoke Island. It's named after the **pirate** Edward Teach—better known as Blackbeard. He's most famous for robbing ships . . . and haunting Teach's Hole.

Blackbeard the pirate during a battle at sea

In 1718, after a long battle at Teach's Hole, sailors captured Blackbeard. They cut off his head, hung it on their ship, and threw his body into the sea. **Legend** says that the body swam around the ship three times, looking for its head. Today, a strange light is sometimes seen under the water. Many people think it's Blackbeard's headless ghost.

Sometimes, on stormy nights near Teach's Hole, people report hearing a voice. It sounds like someone shouting, "Where's my head?"

Phantom in Pink

The Grove Park Inn, Asheville

The Grove Park Inn first opened in 1913. Many famous people have stayed there. But the most famous guest of all is a ghost!

For 100 years, the ghost has appeared in the hotel. The **spirit** is often seen as a young woman in a pink ball gown—or as a pink mist. She is said to have been a hotel guest in the 1920s. Some say she fell to her death from a fifth-floor window.

The Grove Park Inn

The Pink Lady appears to love children. Her ghost has been seen at the beds of sick kids. The spirit comforts them and holds their hands.

A doctor once stayed at the hotel with his family. When he left, he asked the hotel staff to thank the lady in the pink dress. He said that his children had really enjoyed playing with her.

The Pink Lady is often seen in room 545. This may have been where she stayed before she died.

The Red-Eyed Beast

Highway 194, Valle Crucis

A deep howl echoes in the town of Valle Crucis. A pair of glowing red eyes appears. A strange creature is on the hunt.

One moonlit night, two men were driving on Highway 194. Suddenly, something jumped out from behind a **gravestone** in a church cemetery. The driver **swerved** to avoid it. The men saw what looked like a dog. However, it was no ordinary dog.

The dog was as big as a person. It had spiky black fur and yellow teeth. Its eyes glowed red in the night. The men sped away. The dog chased after the car. Even at 80 miles per hour (129 kph), the beast kept up. It was about to bite the car's bumper when the driver zoomed across a bridge. The creature seemed to disappear. Will it come back on another dark night?

The two men stayed up all night thinking about their terrifying experience.

Spooky Spots in North Carolina

Glossary

fainted (FEYNT-uhd) lost consciousness for a short time

gravestone (GRAYV-stohn) a stone that marks the place where a person is buried

legend (LEJ-uhnd) a story that has been passed down that might not be true

pirate (PIE-ruht) a person who attacks and robs ships at sea

spirit (SPIHR-it) a ghost

supernatural (soo-pur-NACH-ur-uhl) something ghostly or unusual that can't be easily explained

swerved (SWURVD) turned quickly to avoid hitting something

vanished (VAN-ishd) disappeared

wary (WAIR-ee) watchful

Index

Read More

Camisa, Kathryn. *Horror Hotels (Tiptoe Into Scary Places).* New York: Bearport (2017).

Claybourne, Anna. *Don't Read This Book Before Bed: Thrills, Chills, and Hauntingly True Stories.* Washington, DC: National Geographic (2017).

Learn More Online

To learn more about the horror in North Carolina, visit:
www.bearportpublishing.com/ScaryStates

About the Author

Simon Rose is the author of more than 100 books for children and young adults. He loves writing about spooky stuff and tries to be brave when he visits haunted places.